Original title:
Frosty Frolics and Frozen Fiascos

Copyright © 2024 Creative Arts Management OÜ
All rights reserved.

Author: Lila Davenport
ISBN HARDBACK: 978-9916-94-192-8
ISBN PAPERBACK: 978-9916-94-193-5

Shivers and Shenanigans in the Snow

A snowman dressed in silly clothes,
With a carrot nose and crooked toes.
Kids laughing loud, they tumble and roll,
As snowballs fly, they take a stroll.

But wait! A slip, a dive on the ground,
The snowman's head just spun around!
Giggles erupt as the cold winds blow,
In this winter world, the fun is a-go!

Slippery Surprises on Ice

Skates on tightly, balance is key,
Whoosh down the rink, try not to flee.
But oh! A wobble, a slip and a fall,
Everyone's laughing, it's a free-for-all.

A graceful glide, then a sudden twist,
One little pirouette gone amiss.
With toes all tangled, limbs in a fight,
In the chaos of ice, everything's light!

Crystal Dreams and Cumbersome Cascades

The hill shines bright, a glittering sight,
Sleds are ready, oh what a delight!
But wait for a push, and then off they go,
A tumble, a crash, and a face full of snow!

They're all bundled up, but trouble's in store,
One tiny bump sends them rolling once more.
With laughter erupting, and snowmen in queue,
This winter mischief is perfect for two!

Snowbound Shenanigans

In the backyard, a fortress is made,
Igloos and castles, a grand escapade.
With snowflakes falling, they battle and shout,
While hot cocoa waits, all cozy throughout.

Snowballs in hand, then a sneak attack,
But oops! Someone slips, now they're on their back.
Giggles and cheers fill the frosty expanse,
Winter's wild moments give life a grand dance!

Hiccup in the Ice

A penguin slips with a flail,
Down a slope, a quick trail.
With a chuckle, we all see,
Ice can turn clumsy glee.

Snowballs fly from playful hands,
Giggles echo across the lands.
Every tumble, each blunder,
The cracking ice steals the thunder.

Chasing laughter, in winter's glow,
We dance like we don't even know.
A frosty breeze, a raucous cheer,
Clumsiness brings everybody near!

Beneath the Icy Veil

Beneath the shards of crystal bright,
Snowmen wobble left and right.
Carrot noses, crooked grins,
Laughs erupt as winter spins.

A squirrel skids, falls on its back,
Chasing snowflakes in a whack.
With a twirl and a flip, it's clear,
Nature's charm brings endless cheer.

Hot cocoa dribbles down our chins,
We toast to our rather silly wins.
Frosty air and silly pranks,
The snowball fights earn loud thanks!

Laughter Beneath the Snow

Under blankets of fluffy white,
We build our forts with all our might.
Squeals of joy in the frigid air,
Snowy battles without a care.

A tumble here, a splash of cold,
Thrilling tales just waiting to be told.
With icy hats and mismatched socks,
We giggle and slide on snowy blocks.

The winter sun begins to peek,
As cheeks grow pink from laughing weak.
With funny faces and silly tricks,
We dance around amidst the flicks!

Slippery Sagas

On icy trails, we zoom and glide,
With arms outstretched for a wild ride.
A tumble here, a cheer erupts,
As frozen feet get the best of chumps.

An old man slips, his hat takes flight,
We laugh and cheer with sheer delight.
He spins around with a cheeky grin,
Claiming victory where he's been.

Trails of laughter fill the air,
As mischief sparkles everywhere.
In slippery tales, we find our place,
Winter's charm, an endless chase!

Glide of the Snowflakes

Snowflakes dance in the chilly air,
Twisting and turning without a care.
One takes a dive, a bold little twist,
Ending up stuck where the sun doesn't exist.

A troupe of flakes in a spiraled show,
Chasing each other with nowhere to go.
One bumps a tree and giggles in cold,
While others just shiver, their secrets unfold.

Kingdom of Cold

A kingdom built of ice and cheer,
With penguin kings who commandeer.
Sleds go whizzing, oh what a scene,
While snowmen lose hats, looking quite mean.

The frostbitten crown on a queen's frosty brow,
Slips from her head with a mallard's loud "Wow!"
Laughter erupts as it lands in the stew,
Blending in well with the gingerbread crew.

Surreal Slips and Slides

On slippery slopes, we glide and collide,
With giggles and shrieks, what a wild ride!
A plump little squirrel flies past with a squeak,
And lands in a snowdrift without a peek.

Mittens are flung, hats tumble and roll,
As snowballs are thrown with reckless control.
The ground starts to shake as laughter takes flight,
"Who threw that?" "Not me!" in the dazzling white.

Jack Frost's Jamboree

Jack Frost throws parties at midnight so bright,
With icicles draping, a magical sight.
He juggles snowballs and races a hare,
While snow angels giggle, floating without care.

The mistletoe winks as skaters collide,
With bumps and bruises, they courteous slide.
A tumbler twirls, but oh what a flop,
"Let's do it again!" as they all take a drop.

Antarctic Antics

Penguins dancing in a line,
Wobbling like they're out of time.
Sliding much too close, they fall,
Snowballs flying, one and all.

Seals are laughing, what a sight,
Chasing fish with all their might.
Snowmen wobble, start to shake,
Falling over, oh what a break!

A walrus plays a slide guitar,
Underneath the Northern star.
Everyone joins in the fun,
Making memories, one by one.

When the snow starts melting down,
A playful splash in icy ground.
What a winter wonderland,
With laughter echoing on the sand.

Chilled Revelries

Hats and mittens, all askew,
Everyone's a little blue.
But then a snowball flies on by,
We burst out laughing, oh my, my!

Rabbits hop in jackets bright,
Chasing shadows left and right.
A squirrel slips, what a scene,
In the snow, it rolls like cream!

Hot cocoa spills, a mug gone wild,
Kids run laugh like carefree child.
A blizzard comes, a swirling dance,
Who knew winter could enhance?

Frozen fingers, cheeks so red,
Tumbling down, sweets in our head.
What a joy, despite the cold,
Endless tales of laughs retold.

The Great Thaw

Icicles drip like melting dreams,
A river flows, or so it seems.
Sleds now stuck where rivers swell,
Wishing memories we could tell.

Snowmen now begin to fade,
As sunshine's warming serenade.
The puddles wink, a playful glare,
And children jump without a care.

But oops! A splash on grandma's dress,
All in giggles, oh what a mess!
A flock of birds takes silly flight,
Chasing laughter, pure delight.

Woolly hats hang from a line,
The season's end, but aren't we fine?
With tattered hearts and smiles so wide,
We wave goodbye to winter's ride.

Shattered Icicles

An icicle hangs, oh so grand,
An unwary cat, now bland.
With a leap, it gives a shout,
Down it tumbles, roundabout!

Chasing snowflakes, here they go,
With mittened hands, down the slopes, whoa!
Down the hill, a muffled cheer,
Belly flops bring winter near.

A sled goes flying, oh the thrill,
A friendly face, a snowy chill.
Laughter echoes, can't contain,
Snowmen's noses in the rain.

At the end of this frosty spree,
We gather 'round, on knees with glee.
Mom's hot soup is all the rage,
As winter fun takes center stage.

A Delicate Crust

There once was a snowman, quite round,
Who dressed up in clothes he'd found.
His hat flew away,
On a windy day.

With carrots for eyes, he looked grand,
In boots that were two sizes planned.
He slipped on a patch,
Made a comical scratch!

The children all laughed, that was clear,
As he wobbled and spun with such cheer.
He danced with delight,
In the soft moonlight.

Then down came the sun, oh so bright,
He melted away, what a sight!
One puddle remained,
With a smile still gained.

Tales from the Frost

In the woods where the icicles hang,
A squirrel heard laughter and sang.
He slipped on a leaf,
What a comic grief!

The rabbits all gathered, so bold,
To witness a story retold.
With giggles and hops,
They forgot all their crops.

An owl hooted loudly, no doubt,
He joined in the fun, with a shout.
"Whooo, that's the way,
Let's go out to play!"

As dusk painted sky with a blush,
The animals raced in a rush.
With tales that won't end,
Their laughter, our friend.

Winter Wanderlust

A penguin decided to roam,
To find himself far from home.
With flippers so wide,
He slid down the side.

He found a small igloo, quite neat,
Where seals joined him, sharing a treat.
They laughed and they cheered,
As snowflakes appeared.

They danced on the ice with such flair,
Spinning 'round without any care.
With a slip and a spin,
They laughed through the din.

As sunset melted the skies to a glow,
They waved to their friends down below.
In wintery wonder,
They forgot all their blunders.

Twinkling Tundra Tides

At night in the tundra, stars spark,
A fox tried to dance in the dark.
With a trip and a fall,
He giggled through all.

The snowflakes were swirling with glee,
As he rolled on the ground, just to see.
His tail gave a flick,
In a magical trick.

A moose joined him, hoping to prance,
Both laughed as they started to dance.
With a kick and a hop,
They almost did stop.

But the rhythm was strong, oh so sweet,
With each snowy step, they found beat.
On that frosty night,
They conquered with light.

Icicle Dreams

In the chill of the night,
Icicles dangle bright,
They glitter like stars,
After long winter's fight.

The snowman starts to dance,
In a hilarious prance,
His carrot nose wobbles,
Taking a frosty chance.

The penguins all slide down,
With laughter they abound,
In a flurry of snow,
Joyful chaos is found.

Oh, these dreams made of ice,
With each slip and each slice,
Chasing snowflakes with glee,
Oh, what a funny paradise!

Serpentine Snooze

A snowy snake does glide,
With a wiggly, wild ride,
He snoozes in a heap,
While we watch, open-eyed.

Chasing tails, they all laugh,
Winter's silly giraffe,
Wobbling on frosty legs,
Trying hard, but not half!

The frost gets in their fur,
The penguins begin to purr,
Slipping on sleet so slick,
Winter's furry stir.

Under blankets of white,
They tumble through the night,
In a dance of delight,
Oh, what a charming sight!

Mirth of the Icy Realm

In a realm where ice sings,
And laughter rushes like springs,
The snowflakes float and twirl,
Where everyone's joy clings.

A snowball fight breaks out,
With squeals and happy shouts,
A frosty face doused bright,
Laughter weaves all about.

Chasing each other 'round,
With frosty leaps and bound,
The icy wind does giggle,
As smiles in cold resound.

Here in the chilly air,
We toss our worries where,
Letting mirth flow like streams,
In this frosty affair!

Frozen Footloose

The ice rink calls us near,
With skates and grins, not fear,
We slide and trip and spin,
With laughter filling ear.

A tumble here and there,
With silly frosty flair,
The snowflakes dive and dive,
In joyous, icy air.

Shuffling feet, then a slip,
A frosty friendship trip,
In laughter we etch memories,
As the icicles drip.

Whirls of snowflakes and glee,
Winter's funny decree,
We'll dance 'til the sun's light,
In a frosty jubilee!

Playful Frostfall

In a land where snowflakes twirl,
Kids in mittens dash and swirl.
Snowmen rise with crooked grins,
While dogs chase tails in frigid spins.

Hot cocoa spills, laughter's loud,
Snowball battles draw a crowd.
Slip and slide with joyful screams,
Chasing winter's wacky dreams.

Sleds collide and topple over,
Chasing echoes of a clover.
Frosty bites at noses red,
But joy is where our hearts are led.

Snowflakes dance like wild confetti,
In this winter wonder, oh so petty.
Amid the chill, our spirits soar,
In snowy fun, we yearn for more.

A Blizzard of Bliss

A windy gale, a snowstorm's rage,
We bundle up, step on stage.
A flurry of laughter fills the air,
With frozen cheeks and windblown hair.

Snowdrifts deep as chocolate cakes,
Every step a dent, it shakes.
We toss around those fluffy spheres,
And hide behind, embracing fears.

Squeals of joy, a fumble and fall,
A snowy hill becomes our wall.
Fingers numb but spirits bright,
In this madness, pure delight.

As snowflakes fail to land with grace,
We dance in circles, a silly chase.
In winter's whim, we find our glee,
A blizzard's charm, just you and me.

Shivering Shenanigans

Bundled tight in scarfs and hats,
We tumble into snow like cats.
With each flake that kisses our skin,
A giggle escapes, it's where we begin.

A zip and a zoom down icy trails,
Carving our path with hoots and wails.
Mittens toss like confetti bright,
In snowball fights, we reignite.

Chilly air, but our hearts are warm,
Inventing games, a winter charm.
Sliding sideways, we fall and roll,
Amidst the chaos, we find our soul.

Snowmen wobble with sloppy hats,
A dance with yetis and silly pats.
In frozen moments, our spirits thrive,
With icy laughter, we come alive.

Icebound Improv

On the lake, we glide with flair,
Unscripted moves, a chilly dare.
Spinning twirls and leaps galore,
Pinging laughter, we want more!

Snowflakes giggle from the sky,
As we tumble down, oh my, oh my!
With twigs for skis and rocks for goals,
We create mischief that never slows.

Chilly toes and frosty breath,
In this game, we laugh at death.
Every slip, a spontaneous cheer,
In winter's dance, we persevere.

From ice-bound jokes to flurries bright,
We conjure joy from winter's bite.
Here's to fun and the mess we make,
In frozen fields, our hearts awake.

The Chaotic Symphony of Snowfall

Snowflakes twirl in wild delight,
A dance of chaos, pure and light.
Snowmen wobble, noses askew,
As kids launch snowballs, aim askew.

A sled takes flight from a snowy hill,
Riders scream, but it's all a thrill.
Laughter echoes through the air,
As winter's wonders spark our flair.

Hot cocoa spills—what a disaster!
The dog leaps in, running faster.
With snowflakes stuck upon its nose,
It chases joy where the blizzard blows.

Winter's Playful Pranks

Icicles dangle, a frosty tease,
As snowflakes land with the greatest ease.
A frozen puddle, a slip and slide,
While cheeky squirrels scamper wide.

Snowballs ready, a sneaky plan,
Launch them quick—oh, here comes Stan!
Caught unaware, he tumbles down,
In fluffy white, he wears a crown.

The dog in boots, a sight to see,
Trots through snow, all carefree.
With every leap, it makes a splash,
Chasing snowmen, oh what a crash!

Echoes of Laughter in the Chill

Chattering teeth beneath the moon,
We gather 'round to sing a tune.
Past the pines and frosted trees,
Our giggles dance upon the breeze.

A snowball fight, it's quite a sight,
Projectiles flying—oh, what delight!
In wobbly boots, we glide and slide,
As snowflakes twirl, we run with pride.

A pine tree bows, heavy and low,
Beneath the weight of winter's show.
And laughter erupts like a snow-capped wave,
In our hearts, joy is what we crave.

Flurries of Fun in the Winter Glow

Twinkling lights on rooftops shine,
In the chill, we toast with wine.
A dance of snowflakes with a twist,
Winter's magic, none can resist.

A friendly snowman, hat askew,
With a carrot nose and eyes so blue.
Children giggle, try to pose,
With snowballs flying—who knows where it goes?

The air is crisp, the laughter loud,
As we tumble into snowy clouds.
With friends beside, we stomp and play,
In this wonderland, we'll laugh away.

The Snowball Chronicles

A snowball fight in our back yard,
When I slipped and fell, it hit me hard.
My friends all laughed, they couldn't believe,
That I turned into snowman, I took a reprieve.

Snow piled high, like an icy wall,
We built it up and made a tall.
But when the dog dashed right through,
Our tower fell, oh what a view!

In winter's chill, we took our aim,
Each throw we practiced, a snowy game.
But one frozen lump flew out of sight,
And hit an old teacher, what a fright!

With laughter ringing, and cheeks so red,
We all agreed, it was worth the spread.
The snow may melt, and summer appear,
But those snowball tales will linger here.

Icy Escapades

On a slick patch near the old oak tree,
I tried to skate, but oh dear me!
With a perfect glide, I took a chance,
But ended up in a wild dance!

My brother chuckled, hiding behind,
A snowdrift plush, he was so blind.
I aimed a throw, but missed him near,
And hit Mom's flowers with icy cheer.

We built a fort, our winter pride,
Then saw a squirrel, oh how we tried!
He stole our stash, our snack attack,
And left us cold, we took it back!

Sliding down hills, with giggles so wide,
We fell in heaps, the snow our guide.
With joy and laughter, the day flew by,
Making frozen memories as the clouds rolled by.

Blur of White Laughter

A snowy day filled with cheer,
We rolled some balls, had no fear.
But one went rolling, oh what a race!
It knocked down Dad, right in place!

My sister spun with joyful shout,
While snowflakes danced, swirling about.
We chased each other, fast and silly,
Until someone tripped, oh what a frilly!

Sledding down, a bumpy ride,
Me and my pals, slipping side to side.
We crashed in laughter, then got stuck,
A messy heap, with some bad luck!

But in that moment, all that we shared,
Was joy and fun, none had a care.
For in the blur of the winter's gaze,
We found our laughter in frozen ways.

Frozen Mischief Makers

In the park we gathered three,
To concoct some chills and glee.
But while planning, slipped on ice,
And landed hard - not once, but twice!

A little dog thought it was a game,
He joined in too, oh what a claim!
With trails of snow behind his feet,
He sent us tumbling to the street!

We threw back snow with all our might,
But someone shouted, a silly fright!
A car came by, we froze in shock,
As it splashed us with a flurry block!

But with each prank and plenty of fun,
We knew our day had just begun.
For in the chill, we found delight,
In silly moments, all day and night!

Sliding into Mischief

A snowy slope, the ice is slick,
With every slide, I feel the kick.
My hat takes flight, my scarf's a kite,
Oh, what a laugh, such pure delight.

Down the hill, I flip and flop,
In a tangle, I come to a stop.
My friends all giggle, can't contain,
As I roll like a snowball, oh, what a pain!

Snowballs fly, a daring throw,
But I miss my mark, and oh, the woe!
Instead of winning, I take a spin,
And land face-first — let the fun begin!

With cheeks aglow and laughter loud,
I stand up tall, part of the crowd.
In this wintry playground, we dance and cheer,
Creating chaos, year after year!

Frostbitten Folly

The sun shines bright on the frozen lake,
With ice skates strapped, I take the break.
But wobbly legs, a comic sight,
I twist and turn, then take flight!

My buddy laughs, he slips and slides,
In a frosty battle, nobody hides.
Snowmen cheer as we tumble and roll,
We're out for fun; that's the ultimate goal!

A snowball war, we start to create,
But the ice gives way — oh, isn't fate great?
With giggles erupting from every hole,
We find ourselves buried, oh, what a hole!

As the day fades, and dusk comes near,
We head back home, but still, we cheer.
For every folly in the frosty air,
Is a mem'ry made, our laughter to share!

Winter's Whimsy

The flurry swirls, a playful game,
With little feet, and no one to blame.
Chasing snowflakes, we leap and shriek,
In this chilly dance, it's laughter we seek.

A gentle push, we tumble down,
The snow is soft; no fear to frown.
With noses red and cheeks aglow,
Each frosty prank puts on a show!

Hot cocoa waits for us inside,
But first, let's see who'll take the ride.
A wooden sled, a hill so steep,
Our shrieks of joy, so wild, so deep!

Let winter's wonders take us away,
As we revel in games till end of day.
For in every slip and every fall,
Is a giggle shared, enchanting us all!

Glimmering Glaciers

In the distance, the icebergs gleam,
A frosty fantasy, like a dream.
We dance with penguins, slide with glee,
In this frozen wonder, so wild and free.

A ice-castle built, oh, what a feat,
With lopsided towers, it's quite a treat.
We throw in some snow for that extra charm,
But it collapses — oh, no harm!

With jokes in tow, we make our way,
To the slippery pond where we love to play.
A slip, a slide, then a grand belly flop,
Laughter erupts, we just cannot stop!

When day turns to night, our cheeks so bright,
We reminisce on our frosty flight.
In every moment, mischief does rise,
Wrapped up in joy, beneath winter skies!

Crisp Adventures

In the meadow, snowflakes twirl,
Sledding dreams start to unfurl.
But a tumble sends me flying,
Oh, how I'll keep on crying!

Hot cocoa spills, marshmallows drift,
With each sip, I catch a lift.
But a snowball found my nose,
And now I'm a frozen rose!

Chasing penguins on a spree,
I slipped and bounced off a tree.
Laughter echoes in the night,
As shadows dance in pure delight!

Snowman's hat goes flying high,
Off it sails, like birds in sky.
With laughter ringing loud and clear,
We fashion snowmen, cheer and cheer!

Luminous Laughter

Beneath the stars, the snowflakes gleam,
We try to catch them, what a dream!
But they slip right through our hands,
Leaving only frosty strands.

A penguin slides upon his rear,
That silly bird brings lots of cheer!
With flippers flapping in the breeze,
He's off again—what fun to tease!

Carrots tossed, a snowman's stare,
Wait, where's his nose? It's gone somewhere!
We search and hunt all over town,
Only to find it in a frown!

Laughter fills the chilly air,
As cheeks grow rosy, hearts laid bare.
Our winter fun, a merry tale,
While snowflakes dance like tiny sails!

Wintertime Revelations

Each snowy patch is a perfect slide,
But hidden rocks must be defied!
One wrong turn, a flurry of yells,
As down we go, oh what hells!

A frozen pond, so slick and sly,
With every step, we laugh and cry.
A tumble here, a splash there too,
Our laughter rings, what a hullabaloo!

Finding mittens lost in snow,
An epic quest, how much we know!
With every scoff and every cheer,
We spin and roll with winter's leer!

Nosedive into a snowbank deep,
Who knew that winter fun could leap?
With giggles shared, we'll never stop,
Our joyful hearts will always pop!

Avalanche of Joy

We built a mountain, quite the sight,
But down it came with all its might!
A rumble loud, a snowy crash,
Who knew that fun could turn to splash!

With snowflakes caught in hair and hats,
We toss and play like furry cats.
The frozen ground is quite a friend,
For every slip, there's laughter's bend!

In snowball fights, we throw with glee,
But I got hit—oh, woe is me!
Surprise attacks from sneaky hands,
Leave us all in playful bands!

At day's end, with cheeks aglow,
We gather 'round for tales to stow.
With goofy grins and hearts so light,
We cherish snow days, pure delight!

Enchanted in White

In a wonderland covered in snow,
Snowmen wobble, their hats won't stay low.
Sleds zoom past like shooting stars,
While penguins plot snowball wars!

Laughter echoes, a delightful cheer,
As snowflakes dance, bringing good cheer.
Kids trip over, then burst out in giggles,
While dogs chase tails in joyous wiggles!

A snowflake lands on a warm nose,
It sneezes loud, everyone knows.
Hot cocoa spills as cups collide,
In this frozen land, we all abide!

With snowball fights and chilly glee,
Laughter lingers, wild and free.
This white wonder, a playful sight,
Where chilly dreams bring pure delight!

Cascading Winter Joy

Hats fly off in a frosty breeze,
With every snowflake, we all freeze.
Slipping, sliding, what a sight!
Laughing hard with all our might!

Rabbits hop, their ears like sails,
Chasing shadows, leaving trails.
There's a chill in the air, it's clear,
Then someone yells, 'Hey, I'm right here!"

Bright red cheeks and snotty noses,
Rolling in snow, a game of poses.
Snow angels stretch across the ground,
Laughter erupts, oh what a sound!

The hills are alive with screech and shout,
As winter fun erases doubt.
With every tumble, a laugh will grow,
In this winter land, let joy overflow!

Glacial Glimpses

Icicles dangle from rooftops high,
As neighbors wave, then slip, oh my!
Dogs do zoomies, tails a blur,
While kids get stuck in snowdrifts, for sure!

Snowballs fly through the chilly air,
A direct hit—oh, who would dare?
With cheeks aglow, we run and play,
Even the grumpy join today!

The snowman's grin is wider than wide,
But a rogue snowball knocks him aside.
He topples down with a mighty crash,
We burst into giggles—a joyous splash!

Every flake seems to laugh and dance,
In this frozen world, we take our chance.
For in this chill, we all belong,
In the glacial mirrors, we sing our song!

The Frosted Parade

Parading through with scarves so bright,
In a land where cold feels just right.
Dance of boots in the crisp, white snow,
Watch out below, here comes the show!

Squirrels peep from their icy nests,
As kids wear hats like fuzzy vests.
Piggyback rides down sliding hills,
Squeals of joy, oh what a thrill!

Mittens mismatched, a fashion faux pas,
Yet everyone smiles, it's quite the gala.
Snowflakes tumble, a sparkling crown,
While giggles echo through the town!

In a flurry of fun that seems to bend,
With every laugh, the day won't end.
With cheeks so rosy, we proudly claim,
That every winter brings its own game!

Whims of the Wintry Night

Under the moon, we slip and slide,
Snowballs flying, a playful ride.
A snowman's hat atop my head,
I trip and laugh, fall back instead.

Twinkling lights on every tree,
I whip my friend, she squeals with glee.
Hot cocoa spills upon my face,
We're covered from head to chilly base.

Chasing shadows, we forgot to check,
The icy patch, oh what the heck!
With every tumble, giggles grow,
Our winter bliss put on a show.

Laughter echoes in the night,
While twirling snowflakes take their flight.
The world is bright, our spirits soar,
Who knew the cold could bring such roar?

Silhouettes in Snow

Footprints dance on a snowy trail,
A catapult of laughter's gale.
With every slip, the laughter spreads,
A friend falls softly—what a spread!

Snowmen wink with carrot noses,
As we build, the cold wind dozes.
A sudden shove, and someone's blue,
Snow much fun, we'll never rue!

Racing down the hillside wide,
Sleds collide, we giggle and glide.
With arms outstretched, we tumble down,
A frosty crown, a snowy gown.

Glowing fires and hungry s'mores,
The warmth awaits behind the doors.
We'll tell the tales of our great feats,
In winter's thrall, laughter repeats!

Boundless Blankets of White

Blankets piled, a mountain high,
We burrow deep and peek to spy.
Each crunching step's a sound we love,
A clumsy roll, we laugh enough.

Pine trees dressed in icy gowns,
Tiny snowflakes spin like clowns.
Our cheeks are red, the air is light,
We chase the chill into the night.

Snowflakes twirl as we break out,
With joyful screams, we all shout.
The snowball fight turns everyone canned,
A face full of fluff, nowhere to stand!

As daylight wanes, we gather near,
Hot chocolate here, let's spread the cheer.
The boundless white brings mischief bright,
In every flake, a delight!

The Giggle Glade

In the glade where giggles rise,
Snowmen play with snowy eyes.
A mitten flung, oh what a hoot,
Launching snowballs, who will shoot?

We sculpt a chair, an icy throne,
Where laughter rules and chill is known.
With every splash, we twist and shout,
Rolling laughter, there's no doubt.

Sliding down on cardboard bright,
The joyous cries to fill the night.
We tumble, we spin, like whirlwinds spin,
With every frolic, we just grin.

The stars above in twinkling chat,
As our antics make the night a blast.
In this glade where frolics bloom,
Winter's magic lights the room!

Echoing Giggles in the Snowy Abyss

In a world of white and cheer,
The laughter echoes loud and clear,
Snowballs fly with playful zest,
Each toss a chance to manifest.

Bundled up in woolly gear,
With rosy cheeks, we have no fear,
We tumble down the snowy hill,
Our hearts are light, our spirits thrill.

Whispers of snowflakes dance around,
As we spin and tumble, laughter bound,
A snowman waves with frosty hands,
While we plot mischief in snow-filled lands.

Through snowdrifts deep and puddles cold,
Each frolic is a story told,
Our giggles fill the winter air,
In this icy world, we laugh and share.

The Slip and Slide of Joyous Journeys

Sliding down on sleek, slick ice,
With open mouths, we shout, 'Oh, nice!'
A tumble here, a giggle there,
Wobbling legs show little care.

Socks just aren't meant for this game,
One wrong move, oh what a shame!
Rolling in snow, we can't contain,
The giggles mixed with minor pain.

Chasing friends makes winter bright,
Their squeals and slips are pure delight,
A wild ride, a twisty turn,
The art of falling, we must learn.

With frozen noses and bright blue skies,
We spin around as snowflakes fly,
Each joyful slip, a fleeting thrill,
In these frosty fields, we have our fill.

Frozen Larks and Mischievous Moments

In the air, a snowball flies,
Zooming past with squeals and sighs,
Laughter bubbles, joy ignites,
As playful spirits reach new heights.

A daring leap from frosty heights,
Into soft mounds, oh what sights!
Face first in flakes, oh what a scene,
We get up laughing, all shiny and clean.

Chasing shadows, dodging spry,
A friendly snowball fight nearby,
With giggles spilling, oh what fun,
As day and night blend into one.

Each frosty prank, a playful tease,
With laughter ringing through the trees,
In a world so cold, so bright,
Moments of joy warm up the night.

The Winter Wager: Who Will Slip?

Gather round, let's make a bet,
Who among us will win this set?
With courage high, we take a stand,
On this slippery and icy land.

A leap, a slide, a twisting fate,
Who will stumble, who'll celebrate?
The laughter builds, the wagers soar,
Each slip and slide is worth much more.

As socks and boots clash in the race,
A soaked behind, a snowy face,
With every tumble, cheers still rise,
We revel in each funny surprise.

So gear up tight, the game's on now,
Will you join or take a bow?
In this winter wonder, laughter glows,
As we all chase the bliss that flows.

Mirth in the Mists

Chilling laughter fills the air,
As snowflakes dance without a care.
A slide down hills, oh what a sight,
Wrapped in layers, warm and bright.

Carrots grin from snowman faces,
Sleds go flying, wild embraces.
Fingers cold but hearts are warm,
Winter's joy is a charming swarm.

Icicle Enigmas

Dripping secrets from the eaves,
Icicles sway like winter thieves.
Catch a glimpse of melting charms,
As laughter echoes, spreading warms.

Puddles form in silly tricks,
Splashes come with playful kicks.
With every slip, a giggle grows,
In winter's grip, the fun just flows.

Whispering Winds of Winter

Whispers swirl in frosty breath,
Gentle nudges, life and jest.
As snowflakes twirl in wild ballet,
Nature's joke in a grand display.

A friendly snowball finds its mark,
Lively chuckles in the park.
With each throw, the world ignites,
In frozen fun, where joy delights.

Snowy Soiree

Gather round for laughter's call,
Snowball fights and joyful brawl.
Hot cocoa warms the chilly hands,
While chalky snow drifts make new lands.

Tracks of laughter trail behind,
Winter's love so sweet and kind.
In this wonderland so bright,
Chase the snowflakes, pure delight.

Merry Mishaps in the Land of Ice

A snowman with a crooked nose,
Danced in circles, wearing clothes.
He tripped on his own icy feet,
Then tumbled down, oh what a feat!

The penguins held a sliding race,
Each one vying for first place.
But slippery snow, so fresh and bright,
Sent them flying with pure delight!

A snowball fight began to brew,
With giggles, shouts, and laughs that flew.
But wait! A snowball hit a dog,
Who barked and chased through fog and smog!

Though mishaps came, they would not frown,
With every slip, they spun around.
In this chilly land full of cheer,
They're always laughing, year to year!

Enchanted Snowflakes in Playful Pursuit

Snowflakes danced like scattered dreams,
 Twirling down with silvery beams.
 Caught in laughter, caught in glee,
 Chasing each other, wild and free!

A curious squirrel donned a hat,
 Slinked around, just like a cat.
 He leapt, he gleamed, he took a fall,
 Landed right in a snowball!

Ice slides turned into a grand parade,
 Where everyone tried to serenade.
 But one brave soul lost his grip,
 And down the slope, took quite the trip!

The air was filled with giggles bright,
 As friends united, what a sight!
 In this land of cold and fun,
 The laughter sparkles, never done!

Chill in the Air

A frosty breeze began to swirl,
As snowflakes danced, a lovely twirl.
But one glimmering flake lost its way,
And landed right on a kid at play!

Hot cocoa spilled from a clumsy hand,
As laughter filled the winter land.
The marshmallows bounced off the snow,
Creating fluff wherever they'd go!

The sled was stuck in a snowy heap,
While giggling friends began to creep.
One tiny shove sent it all askew,
And down the hill they wildly flew!

Yet in the chill, there bloomed some cheer,
As mishaps turned to funny jeers.
With chill in the air and smiles so wide,
Winter won't stop this joyful ride!

Icebound Whispers

Whispers of fun drape the white land,
Where frosty giants make their stand.
A towering snowman loomed so large,
But fell with a bounce, now that's a charge!

Bubbles frosted in the chill breeze,
Popped with a giggle and a freeze.
Chasing them down, kids in a race,
Slipping and sliding all over the place!

A dog on skates had quite the flair,
But ended up tangled in a chair.
The laughter spread from ear to ear,
As icebound whispers filled the sphere!

With each little blunder under the skies,
They found joy in each other's eyes.
In this wintry world, full of sights,
It's the laugh that makes the heart take flight!

Chill Whispers in the Moonlight

In the night, snowflakes dance,
They giggle and twirl, what a chance!
A snowman winks with a carrot nose,
As the chill tickles, and laughter grows.

Little critters slide on ice,
Squeaking joyfully, oh, how nice!
A squirrel slips, then takes a leap,
In the moonlight, secrets creep!

Snowballs fly through the shiny air,
Faces painted with frosty flair.
Laughter echoes, a playful jest,
In the winter, we find our best.

With every twist, and every turn,
There's joy in frozen, we always learn.
A frosty world, so bright and clear,
Whispers of mischief, full of cheer.

Icy Adventures Beneath the Stars

Under stars, where icicles gleam,
A penguin waddles, it's quite the dream!
Slide down hills, a big snowball fight,
Chasing each other, what pure delight!

Snow boots stuck in a snowy glop,
A laugh erupts, then a belly flop.
Make a snow angel, then roll away,
Winter's playtime, oh what a day!

As we stumble, slip, and glide,
Cheeks all rosy, we smile wide.
Hot cocoa waits by the crackling fire,
Our hearts, like snowflakes, never tire.

The stars above, they twinkle bright,
As we recount our silly flight.
In this chilly, joyful spree,
Every moment is pure glee!

Glacial Games and Glistening Trails

In the field, where snowflakes sprout,
Laughter echoes, join the shout!
With sleds that zip down frosty hills,
Each turn a thrill, a rush that thrills.

A snowball flies and hits a hat,
Who threw that one? It's all a spat!
Giggles bubble, as we retreat,
Rolling in snow, oh, what a treat!

The evening glows with frosty lights,
Crafting a snow fort for epic fights.
Crouched down low, with stealth so sly,
We plot our launch of snow from high.

Snowmen rise, with eyes aglow,
Whispering secrets only we know.
In this winter, our hearts entwine,
With warmth and laughter, all feels divine!

Winter's Gleeful Gambols

With every stomp on crunchy snow,
A playful giggle, off we go!
Building dreams of icy wonder,
In freezing air, we laugh and thunder.

Snowflakes tickle against our skin,
Chasing joy, let's all jump in!
Each little slip brings gleeful yells,
In frosty breath, our spirit swells.

An icy slide, a game of bold,
Tales of bravado, soon retold.
Embracing winter's chilly charm,
With every giggle, we build and farm.

A world of frost, a playful spree,
Together we sing, wild and free.
In every toss, and every twirl,
Winter's spirit wraps the world.

Twirls and Tumbles in White Wonderland

In the snowy land where we stomp and glide,
Children chatter, their laughter can't hide.
With a push on the sled, off we go with a squeal,
Over snowbanks we fly, oh what a thrill!

We tumble and roll, make snow angels with glee,
A snowball flies past; oh, look out for me!
Chasing each other through powdery drifts,
The best kind of fun; it surely uplifts.

Hot cocoa awaits, warm inside we'll stay,
But for now, let's conspire in games far away.
With noses so red and mittens askew,
We'll create some new chaos, there's much still to do!

As dusk starts to fall, our breath clouds in air,
We laugh at our antics, without a care.
A dance with the snowflakes, we shimmy and spin,
In this winter wonderland, let the fun begin!

Crystalline Capers and Daring Delights

A slip on the ice, oh, what a mad dash,
Laughter erupts as we land with a crash.
Our snowman wobbles, it's got quite a hat,
But he's all smiles, imagine that!

Skates on our feet, we glide and we twirl,
A pirouette gone wrong? Give it a whirl!
With giggles and grins, we tumble around,
The joy of our jest echoes loud with a sound.

Snowflakes are gently like feathers that fall,
We gather them up into a fluttering ball.
Caught in a flurry, our cheeks all aglow,
Our day turns to laughter in this dazzling show!

A daring jump now, who will go first?
We pile up the snow, the excitement's immersed.
With shrieks and some shoves, in this frosty delight,
Every mishap makes memories, oh what a sight!

Winks of Ice and Sprightly Winter

The trees painted white with a wink of the night,
We race down the slope, pure joy in our flight.
With a hiccup and tumble, we scatter and yell,
Each fall brings new laughter; it's truly a spell!

Snowflakes like diamonds dance in the air,
A friendly snowball finds a hat that we share.
Our cheeks are all rosy, our spirits so bright,
In this whimsical world, winter feels just right.

With sleds made of laughter, we glide with a cheer,
The snowman is watching, his grin wide and clear.
We clap at our antics, the moments so sweet,
As we twirl and we tumble on ice-capped concrete!

So here we will play, let the day never end,
In this magical realm, each curve is a friend.
With ice and with giggles, we create our own song,
In this land of good humor, we feel we belong!

Sparking Joy in the Snowy Fields

In the snowy expanse where the wild giggles ride,
We dash to the hill, feeling joy as our guide.
With sleds made from cardboard, we launch and we land,
In fits of pure laughter, we frolic on sand!

A mishap with snow, there's a blizzard of fun,
Each slip brings a chuckle; oh, we've just begun!
We gather our friends for a snowball surprise,
With shouts of delight, we aim for the skies!

The frost on our noses, the snugness within,
The smell of hot chocolate, a warm winter's win.
Each caper we chase, our spirits so light,
With whimsy and giggles, we dance through the night!

As evening descends, we'll trot home with glee,
With stories to tell, oh, how happy we'll be.
In this land of enchantment, where laughter's the key,
The joy of the season forever feels free!

Polar Playdates

Little penguins skitter about,
Chasing snowflakes, what a rout!
They tumble, they roll, like a ball,
A slippery slide turns into a sprawl.

In woolly hats, they jump and play,
Creating snowmen that sway and sway.
They slip on ice, give a shriek,
But laughter's the prize they seek!

Snowball fights with giggly squeals,
Waddling around in boots like heels.
An ice rink formed by a frozen stream,
They twirl and glide like in a dream.

As day turns to night, stars appear,
They gather 'round, sharing cheer.
Hot cocoa waits at the end of fun,
Polar playdates, oh what a run!

Sledding into Laughter

Down the hill, they zip with glee,
Who knew sledding was so free?
A tumble here, a flip or two,
Giggles float like laughter dew.

The snowflakes dance upon their cheeks,
Racing into sunny peaks.
Sleds collide, a bundle of joy,
With every crash, a gleeful oy!

Falling back, they lay in white,
Making angels, oh what a sight!
Sticks for wings, or snow for hair,
Sledding shenanigans everywhere!

As twilight glows, they pack it in,
With cheeks all rosy, smiles that win.
Tomorrow's sledding calls their name,
For laughter always stirs the flame!

Secrets of the Snowfall

Whispers of snow, soft and sly,
Falling gently from the sky.
Kids peek out, with eyes so wide,
To catch those flakes, they run outside!

Snowball secrets hidden deep,
As shadows of winter quietly creep.
With mittens on, they form a wall,
Planning pranks that might just enthrall.

A snowman wears a carrot nose,
But someone plops a hat that glows!
The laughter rings, a cheerful sound,
As snowball tricks leave smiles all around.

But as the sun begins to fade,
The secrets of snow are surely made.
They bundle up, with hearts so light,
Dreaming of mischief, in the moonlight!

Crystal Capers

Sparkling crystals, gleaming bright,
Adventures waiting in the cold night.
With twinkling eyes, they dance and spin,
In snow-suit capes, let the fun begin!

Puppies leap in sparkling snow,
Chasing tails, oh what a show!
Snowflakes twirl, a circus act,
With every leap, it's a giggle-packed!

Ice skates slip, a wobble here,
Someone's down—oh dear, oh dear!
But in the laughter, no one minds,
Joyous chaos is what one finds!

As night falls softly on the land,
They build a fort and take a stand.
With crystal capers to ignite,
They'll dream of joy till morning light!

Fumbles Amongst Frosted Pines

In a snowy glade, a squirrel slips,
Down the driver's side, he does flips.
A chorus of giggles, from birds up high,
As he tumbles and stumbles, oh me, oh my!

A frosty branch gives the dog a fright,
He jumps back quick, then bolts out of sight.
His tail's a flag in the chilly breeze,
Chasing shadows among the trees.

Children in sleds race down the hill,
One topples over; what a thrill!
Snowballs fly, laughter fills the air,
A war of wit, no one's too spare!

As snowmen stand with crooked hats,
One falls over, rolling like a cat.
With giggles galore, they flee the mishap,
Winter's charms in a snowflake wrap.

A Dance of Frost and Fun

Under twinkling lights, kids start to sway,
With mittened hands, they clap and play.
The ice beneath is hardly sound,
But everyone laughs as they spin around.

A grownup slips, with arms held wide,
He crashes down, and then he slides.
With rosy cheeks and beaming grins,
They help him up, and let the fun begin!

A snowman winks with a cheeky grin,
His stick arms wave as the dance begins.
Around and around, they twirl and soar,
On this frosty floor, who could ask for more?

Giggles and gasps as toes feel the chill,
They dart away, but return for the thrill.
Each giggling stumble becomes a sweet song,
In a world where laughter just can't go wrong.

Sliding on a Whimsy's Edge

A slide so tall, a dare is made,
With bated breath, adrenaline played.
One cheers loudly, takes the leap,
And lands in snow, a dive, not deep!

Come see the ducks on a frozen lake,
Waddling sideways, no need to break!
They quack in surprise when one takes a dive,
Flipping and flapping, oh how they thrive!

On tiny hills, kids gather in rows,
Ready, set, go! Down each one flows.
But wait! A rogue sled flies in with a zoom,
And chaos erupts; laughter fills the gloom.

As the sun sets low, colors blend bright,
The day's mishaps add to their delight.
With cheeks aglow from the chill and the cheer,
They dream of the next frosty, fun-filled year.

Cold Kisses and Laughter Trails

Snowflakes dance like love letters sent,
Landing sweetly, a magical event.
With cold kisses on noses, and warmth in hearts,
They weave through the woods, chasing playful parts.

An oversized scarf tangles the crowd,
As everyone giggles and gathers loud.
One takes a trip and lands in a bush,
A flurry of laughter in the snowy hush.

Snowball battles break out like a storm,
With every toss, the giggles warm.
With red noses and cheeks aglow,
The cold can't freeze the warmth they show.

As shadows grow long and the stars appear,
They gather 'round tales that bring them cheer.
In the moonlit night, they'll laugh and play,
Until frosty dreams chase the day away.

The Adventures of a Snowflake's Journey

Once a flake from clouds above,
Danced in air, a twisty shove.
Twirled and spun without a care,
Landed on a dog's cold hair.

The pup took off, a sudden dash,
Caught the flake in a wild splash.
"Catch me if you can!" she cried,
As the snowball fight replied.

Sailed through trees, a mellow glide,
Tickled noses, oh what pride!
Met a friend, a plump snowman,
They plotted, "Let's make snow, man!"

Off they went, a companion's quest,
Into the wind, they were blessed.
Silly games as night drew near,
Each giggle warmer, winter cheer.

Glinting Laughter on the Frozen Lake

Beneath the moon, the surface gleams,
Ice holds secrets, funny dreams.
A skater slips, arms flail in fright,
Splashes laughter, pure delight.

A penguin waddles, takes a slide,
Grinning wide, it does not hide.
"Be careful!" shouts a nearby cat,
But off she goes, just like that!

The ice cracking, a dramatic sound,
Everyone bursts into giggles around.
A seal pops up with a flip,
"Come join me!" says with a quip.

At twilight's end, the fun won't cease,
Each snowball thrown brings joyful peace.
With glinting eyes and frosty breath,
They laugh, forgetting winter's heft.

Sliding into Laughter

Down the hill, a thrilling ride,
With cheeks so red, they can't abide.
Off they zoom, a yelp, a cheer,
Shouts of joy that all can hear.

One bounced high, a graceful flip,
Landed hard, but still a trip.
Covered in snow, they roll around,
Giggling loud with laughter's sound.

A snowball formed in hand, not shy,
To toss and dodge, that's the guy!
But the wind had plans, oh so sly,
Sent it back, oh my, oh my!

They crumbled down, a pile of fun,
While sunbeams melt and days do run.
Snowmen join in, it's all a game,
In a winter's world, we're all the same.

The Hilarious Outburst of Winter

Winter comes with frosty breath,
Like a jester dancing with depth.
With mismatched socks, children play,
Building castles, hip-hip-hooray!

A squirrel fumbles, drops a nut,
While running fast, it takes a cut.
Straight into a mound, what a sight,
Snowflakes tumble, reaching flight.

A group of friends, they start to sing,
Melodies dance, oh, what a fling.
An owl hoots, "That's out of tune!"
And laughs echo through night's monsoon.

Through whispered winds and chilly glee,
They spin and whirl, just wild and free.
Each snowman smiles with button eyes,
In winter's grip, joy never dies.

Chill and Thrill

Snowflakes dance in wild delight,
Noses red, oh what a sight.
Sleds that fly with reckless cheer,
Fall and bounce, then laugh and jeer.

Hot cocoa spills, what a blend!
Marshmallows float, friends pretend.
With snowball fights, we draw the line,
Then slip and slide on icy wine!

Giggling elves in winter's grasp,
Chasing warmth, we tightly clasp.
In every flake, a silly fate,
Our frozen mischief is first rate!

Chill and thrill, the moments fly,
In raucous joy, we sip and sigh.
As laughter crackles in the freeze,
Winter brings us to our knees!

Tinsel Terrors

Lights that twinkle, but oh so bright,
Caught in branches, a funny sight.
Ornaments roll, they make a dash,
Down the hall, oh what a crash!

Cats on trees, a festive plan,
In their bliss, they skewer a fan.
With a twitch of tails, they leap and pounce,
Through garlands where the gold bows bounce.

Mistletoe hangs, but who will kiss?
Just awkward nods, oh what a miss!
But laughter reigns in the yuletide mess,
'Tis the joy of the season's stress!

Tinsel clings with temporary grace,
As we trip and laugh in the race.
Through tangled lights, we find our cheer,
In chaotic joy, we persevere!

Chilling Capers

Tiny feet in snowmen roll,
Carrot noses, a silly goal.
But with one kick, they topple down,
Rolling snowballs all over town!

Gale winds howl, they steal our hats,
Chasing shadows, just like cats.
We spin and twirl in frosty air,
With scarves that flare, we have no care!

Chillin' cheer with giggles bright,
Snowflakes swirl in pure delight.
A slip, a slide, a playful fight,
Winter's humor—oh what a sight!

Chilling capers, we play at will,
In frosty fun, we feel the thrill.
With every laugh, we chase the cold,
As stories of our pranks unfold!

Frozen Fractals

Patterns weave in icy art,
Nature's brush, a frosty heart.
Fumbles abound while we create,
Snowman heads that just can't wait!

With every flake, a tale recites,
As kids throw snow in chilly fights.
Laughter echoes, beards of frost,
In our antics, we count the cost.

Sleds like rockets zoom and glide,
Over ice, our joy can't hide.
Slippery slopes, a comic scene,
Collisions happen; oh how we scream!

Frozen fractals, the world's our play,
With each gleeful scream, we sway.
In icy fields, our spirits soar,
In silly moments, we all explore!

Milton Keynes UK
Ingram Content Group UK Ltd.
UKHW021350011224
451618UK00023B/235